Original title:
Twilight Fires and Soft Snow

Copyright © 2024 Creative Arts Management OÜ
All rights reserved.

Author: Oliver Bennett
ISBN HARDBACK: 978-9916-94-400-4
ISBN PAPERBACK: 978-9916-94-401-1

Frosted Murmurs of Evening

In the chill where whispers tease,
Snowflakes dance like clumsy bees.
A cat leaps high, slips on the ground,
With a splash, it makes quite the sound.

Two penguins chat on frozen hill,
One tells a joke that gives a thrill.
They chuckle loud, it's quite a sight,
As the moon gives them a warm invite.

Glimmers Beneath a Frosted Sky

Stars twinkle up like frozen ticks,
While ice skaters execute slick tricks.
A snowman grins, his carrot nose,
As a kid throws snow, and off it goes.

Under blankets, the rabbits hide,
While chipmunks race, and then collide.
They roll in snow, a blizzard's friend,
With frosty giggles that never end.

Flames Kiss the Frost

A campfire crackles with flair and jest,
While marshmallows roast, they do their best.
But one takes flight, a sugary kite,
As it lands in the snow, oh, what a sight!

Socks begin to melt near the flame,
One toe says, "This is not the game!"
But the other sings, "Let's take a chance,
With hot cocoa, join this crazy dance!"

Ashen Light Over Powdered Ground

Balloons float above, tied to a sleigh,
While children race, just out to play.
A snowball flies with a giggly shout,
Smacking a snowman—just look at him pout!

The sun dips low, the shadows creep,
As reindeer snack on leftovers deep.
Laughter echoes, the day's reprieve,
In a frosty world, we do believe!

Stars Above the Winter Glow

Frozen cheese on roofs so bright,
Raccoons plotting, what a sight!
Snowflakes drift like little fluff,
Can I catch one? No, that's tough!

Jingle bells on dogs do ring,
Puppy prances, doing a fling!
Hot cocoa spills, a marshmallow dive,
Adventures begin, oh, to be alive!

Ashen Bliss on a Snowy Night

Sleds zoom past with laughter loud,
Children roll, beneath a shroud!
Snowmen wear the silliest hats,
Do they think they're all that?

Hot soup spills on frosty toes,
Oops! That's what the kitchen knows.
While outside, the snowflakes race,
I'm stuck drawing my food's face!

The Dance of Light Against White

Lights twinkle on the roof so high,
Squirrels wink as they rush by.
Tinsel tangled in the trees,
I swear it's trying to tease!

Snowball fights that go awry,
Oops! That dove wants to fly.
Giggling friends in layers thick,
This magic snow, the ultimate trick!

Glowing Whispers in the Snowfall

Footprints lead to paths unknown,
Where munching snowflakes seem to moan.
Chubby cheeks and rosy grins,
Let the snowy games begin!

Sipping cocoa, face aglow,
Muffin crumbs, they steal the show!
Laughter echoes through the night,
Oh, what fun! It feels so right!

Surrendering Light to the Evening Chill

The sun gives a wink, then takes a break,
While shadows grow long, and light starts to shake.
A squirrel in a scarf sings songs of delight,
As day surrenders to the giggles of night.

The clouds wear pajamas, fluffy and grey,
While stars do a jig, 'It's our time,' they say.
The moon pulls a prank, with a grin oh so bright,
Leaving daylight dizzy, it's a comical sight.

The Dance of Heat and Frost

The sun throws a party, while frost starts to freeze,
They tango in silence, with quite a tease.
The heat makes a joke, and the cold starts to laugh,
As flames and ice whirl, forming a gaffe.

A penguin in shades, down by the stream,
Sips hot cocoa, living the dream.
While fireflies stumble, tripping on lights,
Claiming it's warm, 'Feel the heat,' they recite.

When Day Meets Night's Caress

As day pulls the blanket, the sun yawns so wide,
The night grins and knuckles, 'Come, enjoy the ride.'
Owls wear their spectacles, wise with surprise,
While crickets recite their rhymes mid the skies.

The horizon turns orange, like a ripe tangerine,
While laughter erupts from a hedgehog's routine.
The stars gossip softly, 'Have you heard the news?'
While the moon paints the sky in sparkly blues.

Sparkling Ashes on Silken White

With glimmers of warmth on a pillow of white,
The embers are giggling, igniting the night.
A marshmallow tiptoes, avoiding the heat,
While snowflakes play tag with a chirpy defeat.

The blanket descends with a flick of its hand,
As laughter erupts from a jolly snow band.
They build a warm bonfire, roasting cold tales,
While ice skates perform, leaving giggles in trails.

The Glow of Dusk Against Snowy Fields

When the sun dips low, the cows wear shades,
In winter's chill, they strike up parades.
Barely can walk, they slip and they slide,
Making cartwheels on snow, cowboys with pride.

Hats made of snowflakes, scarf of a broom,
They tug on a sled, vroom vroom vroom!
Laughter erupts as they topple and flop,
Herd of the winter, they never will stop.

Snowballs take flight like cannonballs hurled,
While the farmer observes, shaking his world.
With every big splash, a chuckle escapes,
At the sight of those moos in the winter capes.

So come gather round, and join in the fun,
For snow in the dusk means joy has begun.
Let's dance 'round the fire, with marshmallows galore,
While cows do the tango, and beg for some more.

A Wisp of Flame in Frozen Air

It's chilly outside, but we've got a spark,
The snowflakes are laughing at the dog in the park.
Pup leaps in the air, does a backflip so grand,
But lands in a drift that looks like a band.

With a woof and a tumble, he's now a white fluff,
Strutting like royalty, looking quite tough.
The snowman laughs back with a carrot for hair,
While the frostbitten squirrels think it's all quite unfair.

We'll roast marshmallows on sticks made of ice,
As the dog chases shadows, oh isn't that nice?
Each toss in the air results in a slip,
As he flops in the snow with a perplexed little dip.

So gather your friends and let's sing a tune,
The dog's our lead singer, howling at the moon.
With giggles and chuckles, we'll warm up the night,
In this frosty circus where laughter takes flight.

The Quiet Kiss of Heat and Ice

A frosty breeze did sneak and slide,
While ice cream dripped, I tried to hide.
The warmth of sun, it laughed at me,
As I slipped and tripped by the icy tree.

With sticky hands and frozen toes,
I danced in circles, struck silly poses.
The neighbors laughed, they found it grand,
As I twirled around, a snowman planned.

Radiance in a White Silence

The moonlight caught a snowman's grin,
While kids all giggled in a snowball bin.
   They tossed and fell, an epic fight,
   Creating chaos in the silver night.

As snowflakes melted on my nose,
I yelled 'Hooray!' as victory grows.
   Yet with a slip, I lost my cap,
And plopped right down, a snowy nap.

Whispered Comforts of Dusk's Veil

As evening falls and shadows creep,
The cat leaps high, into a heap.
With puffs of whiskers, and snow on paws,
He lands where laughter suddenly draws.

A cocoa cup, now half-filled,
With marshmallows that have spilled.
The warmth inside, it smiles so bright,
While outside frost twinkles in the night.

Ethereal Glow Over Soft Blankets

Wrapped up tight in fluff and fun,
The world outside, a snow-white run.
We build a fortress, strange and tall,
Then realize it might just fall!

With each soft pat, a giggle spills,
As snowflakes whirl, they dance and frill.
In this cozy den, we shout and roar,
Hot cocoa in hand, who could ask for more?

Silhouette of Heat Against a Frost-Laden Canvas

In the kitchen, I tried to cook,
But the ice cream melted, that's not how it should look.
Pancakes stuck to the pot like a frozen tease,
I just wanted breakfast, oh why won't it please?

My socks are dancing with warm fuzzy feet,
While the snowflakes are plotting, making life bittersweet.

A dance-off of warmth, a cold winning fight,
Watch me jiggle and giggle in the frosty twilight.

Chasing Light in a Sea of White

I tried to catch snowflakes with a cup,
But they melted away, I gave up.
Snowmen were built with such great care,
Then came the dog, and it was just unfair!

They turned into puddles with big shiny grins,
"Look at me! I'm water!" they cried in spins.
Meanwhile, I tripped, fell over my feet,
A bumpy ride in my own snowy retreat.

The Glow Beneath a Winter Veil

Under blankets piled high, I found my way,
To hot cocoa dreams in a marshmallow bay.
With a sprinkle of joy and a dash of delight,
I gulped down the sweetness, oh what a night!

The cat's in a hat, looking quite absurd,
Complaining about winter, how very unheard!
With each little purr, she risked a cool fate,
Behold the feline king, in his frosty estate!

Glorious Ember under Frosted Breath

Outside I attempted a winter bonfire,
But all I got was a spark and a choir.
The flames sang a tune, quite odd and wild,
Like a karaoke night for every lost child.

Mittens were lost, I now have a cold hand,
Trying to find warmth in a snow-laden land.
Oh, the tales I'll tell of my wintery plight,
With laughter and warmth, through the chill of the night.

Glowing Threads in Winter's Fabric

In the closet, a jacket grins,
Promising warmth for my frozen limbs.
Yet when I put it on with flair,
I look like a penguin unaware!

My scarf's tangled like a spaghetti mess,
Wrapped too tight, I can barely confess.
But when I venture into the snow,
I'm a fashion icon, or so I believe so!

A beanie perched far too high,
I'm a trendsetter, oh my!
Sledding down hills with a cheerful yell,
Face-first into snow—oh, how swell!

As the sun dips low, I catch a glimpse,
Of marshmallows toast, making me do flips.
Hot cocoa spills, but laughter stays,
Winter's a comedy, in the funniest ways!

Flickers on the Edge of Silence

On the porch, the candles sway,
Buzzing bugs join in the ballet.
Sipping tea, while the cat's on the prowl,
It pounces—oops! Right on the towel!

Stars above twinkle like popcorn,
I chew away, like a season's scorn.
A snowflake lands right on my nose,
I sneeze it away, in comic poses!

A frosty wind, with a goofy grin,
Whispers of laughter where warmth begins.
Like friends at a party, awkward and bright,
We dance in the cold, under soft moonlight.

Winter's stage sets in silence tonight,
But our giggles echo, a pure delight.
Here in the chill, where you might think twice,
Laughter's the flame—oh, isn't it nice?

The Calm Between Heat and Cold

A cozy nook, where two worlds collide,
A dance-off of temps, with no place to hide.
The heater huffs like a sleepy old man,
While outside, snowmen plot the next big plan!

I wear socks that don't match at all,
Yet strut like I own this winter ball.
The thermostat cracks jokes with the fridge,
While I hone my skills on an icy ridge!

Mittens are lost, in a sock's embrace,
As I chase my dog through white's embrace.
But every slip leads to laughter's decree,
Winter's just a stage—a grand comedy!

For in this odd world of contrasts and cheer,
I toast to the warmth that's always near.
Between heat and chill, I laugh till I fold,
For life's quite a jest, in colors bold!

Whispers of Warmth in the Frost

Hot soup steams in a bowl like a charm,
While snowflakes outside dance with alarm.
My spoon dives in like a daring hero,
But spills on my shirt—a fashion zero!

Firewood crackles, its laugh fills the air,
I tell a joke, but it's just not fair.
The cats roll their eyes, patients wearing thin,
While I roast marshmallows—let the fun begin!

Outside, the snowmen argue about hats,
While I slip and slide, like a cat with no mats.
The cold nips my nose, it's a curious tease,
Yet somehow, this chill lacks the effort to freeze.

So here we gather, in laughter and warmth,
Even snowflakes know how to take form.
In this frosty place, with hot chocolate in view,
Every chuckle's a flame, shared by me and you!

Frostbitten Dreams in Glowing Embers

In the frigid night we frolic,
Bouncing like penguins on slick grass.
Our noses red from the cold,
Chasing laughter as moments pass.

Hot cocoa spills, quite the scene,
Marshmallows dive, oh what a splash!
We slip and slide, a frosty queen,
While sipping joy in a chilly bash.

The snowman's hat flies to the sky,
A rogue bird claimed it as their prize.
We laugh till tears warm our eyes,
As winter dreams take wobbly highs.

With hats askew, we strike a pose,
Jokes galore, they never tire.
In winter's grasp, it surely shows,
These chilly nights set hearts afire.

Hearth of Stars in Frozen Air

Gather round the crackling glow,
Where tales of spaghetti are spun.
The marshmallows dance, don't you know?
In this kitchen, we're all just fun.

I tried to roast one on a stick,
But it flopped and lounged like a star.
A caramel eagle took a quick pick,
Flying away like it was bizarre.

At the table, spilling juice,
We giggle loud, making a splash.
A snowman grin—what's the use?
He might as well sit, all dapper and brash.

We toast to warmth, our voices rise,
In merriment that feels like flight.
An ice-capped silliness under skies,
Bringing joy through the frosty night.

Warm Glare on a Shimmering Plain

On a blanket, we roll around,
In snowflakes that twirl like a dance.
The sun winks down, it's quite profound,
Spreading laughter with every chance.

Sledding tips, oh what a mess,
One goes sideways, shouting 'Whoa!'
As giggles bounce, we simply guess,
That winter sports rarely steal the show.

Oranges warm our chilly hands,
While snowballs form, oh what a sight.
In our little kingdom with snowman bands,
We launch our dreams in a frosty flight.

The sun bows low, the fun abounds,
Skiing through dreams with comical flair.
With every laugh, the warmth surrounds,
Sparkling joy in the chilly air.

Snowflakes Whisper the Flame's Secret

Snowflakes giggle as they fall,
Hitching rides on our frosty caps.
A giggling snow-folk playball,
While we dodge chilly, slippery traps.

A strange dance of warmth and chill,
Like penguins twirling at midnight.
With every slip, our spirits fill,
With chuckles bright, a pure delight.

In the distance, a howl so quaint,
The dogs leap, sweaters askew.
They chase their tails without restraint,
Making off with the mitten's view.

With snowflakes whispering by my ear,
And biscuits ready by the fire.
Laughter echoes, there's nothing to fear,
In this cozy chaos we all conspire.

Last Shimmers of Sun on Quiet Drifts

The sun waves goodbye with a wink,
While snowflakes dance, oh don't you think?
They tumble and twirl in the fading light,
Creating a scene that's quite a sight.

A snowman trips, oh what a fall,
His carrot nose rolls, but he can't call!
With snowy giggles and a chilly cheer,
A winter party's starting here!

Cold Meets Warm in an Evening Waltz

Hot cocoa spills in a frosty swirl,
As mittened hands do a silly twirl.
The chilly air can't freeze the fun,
When laughter breaks out as day is done.

Snowflakes join in on the dance,
With jumps and spins, they take a chance.
It's hard to frown while we prance about,
In this quirky, chilly winter bout.

Flickering Lights in a Snowbound Dream

The fairy lights flicker, oh what a show,
As snow drifts down like a soft pillow.
A squirrel leaps by, wearing a grin,
Chasing his tail, where does it begin?

The moon peeks out, a cheeky face,
As snowy fluff fills up the space.
With giggles and squeals in the night,
Who knew winter could feel so bright?

Embracing the Chill of Dimming Rays

The sunset laughs as it cools the day,
With a wink and a nod, it leads the way.
Snowmen in scarves look dapper and neat,
While kids try to dress up their snowball fleet.

A snowball fight—now that's delight!
With icy missives taking flight.
Chill in the air, but hearts are warm,
In the frosty realm, it's quite the charm!

Muted Radiance of the Night

The moon plays peek-a-boo with night,
While squirrels wear socks that fit just right.
Stars giggle like a secret crew,
Twinkling tales of the silly things they do.

Bathtubs float in dreamy streams,
As dreams ride on marshmallow beams.
The crickets dance in top hats and tails,
While owls practice their hilarious wails.

A sneaky fox dons a cloak of gray,
While shadows find new games to play.
Frogs recite poetry in the pond,
Their jumping jests craft a night so fond.

Under the canopy, laughter spins,
As each whimsy finds ways to grin.
The night smells like cookies, baked just right,
Oh, the revelry in this sparkly night!

Coals Beneath a Silver Veil

A fire whispers secrets just for fun,
While marshmallows giggle and try to run.
The sticks argue over who's the best,
As laughter erupts from this cozy nest.

With hats made of leaves, they march in line,
Every critter's grinning, feeling just fine.
The embers pop like popcorn's cheer,
Creating a ruckus for all to hear.

Squirrels drag logs, think they're so tough,
But slip on ice, it's just too rough!
Soon the party's a snowy delight,
With everyone laughing in the pale moonlight.

The coals wink softly 'neath snowy cov'rs,
Holding tales of the night and its plucky lovers.
They'll toast to mischief till the dawn,
With sparkle and giggles, this night goes on!

Luminous Echoes in Winter's Embrace

Balloons float gently in the winter breeze,
While penguins practice their funky freeze.
Snowflakes wear costumes, all sparkly and new,
As rabbits wiggle in scarves of bright hues.

The stars wink down, tossing giggles around,
As a snowman attempts to get off the ground.
His carrot nose slips and bends to the side,
While kids sneak behind him, brimming with pride.

Icicles chime like a kooky bell choir,
Singing nonsense, which never tires.
The snowdogs trot by with delighted yips,
Chasing moon shadows, making playful flips.

In the quiet glow of this winter's scene,
Laughter erupts like a bubbling stream.
Echoes of joy dance through the night,
In this chilly realm, everything feels right!

Nightfall's Gentle Blaze

As the sun nods off with a sleepy sigh,
Fireflies leap, like fairies on high.
A raccoon winks from behind a tree,
His antics shine as bright as can be.

The grasswears dew like tiny bling,
While crickets chirp a cheerful spring.
"Let's party!" sings the owl in his chair,
His pals join in with a fluttering flair.

The blaze flickers in whimsical tones,
Telling tales of faces carved in stones.
The shadows prance, doing silly jigs,
While everyone laughs at the dancing pigs.

As night unfolds with its playful grace,
Each moment's wrapped in a cozy embrace.
With giggles bouncing around like balloons,
Nightfall's gentle glow turns up the tunes!

Celestial Embers on a Snowy Canvas

In the sky, sparks dance, a silly sight,
Snowflakes giggle, in the fading light.
A snowman slips, with a carrot nose,
Laughs echo loud, as the chilly wind blows.

Stars in pajamas, twinkling bright,
While penguins waddle, in pure delight.
Chasing shadows, like cats in a show,
Giggles abound, as the cold winds blow.

Fat squirrels stumble, on their winter quests,
As they battle flakes, in their fluffy vests.
Mittens lost, and scarves tied too tight,
All join the frolic, in the snowy night.

Fireside tales, tickle the mood,
With laughter shared, in a joyful brood.
As laughter lingers, and warmth ignites,
The world turns silly, in frosty delights.

The Warmth of Vanishing Day

As daylight grins, before it departs,
Mischief stirs, in cold little hearts.
A snowball flies, with a giggly shout,
As friends tumble down, in joyful rout.

The sun winks low, with a rosy blush,
While snowflakes whirl, in a graceful hush.
Hot chocolate flows, like laughter in streams,
As marshmallows float, fulfilling sweet dreams.

A parka's too snug, a sock lost its mate,
As snowmen plot, to sneak out a fate.
With noses red, and cheeks all aglow,
They dance in the dark, putting on a show.

Then fireside chairs draw friends near and dear,
With stories that sparkle, and echo with cheer.
A time to remember, warmth in our hearts,
As daylight fades, laughter never departs.

Chill of the Dying Fire

The flame plays tricks, with shadows galore,
While marshmallows roast, but they all hit the floor.
The embers crackle, like jokes in the air,
As we share funny tales, without a care.

The moon peeks in, with a glint in its eye,
While snowflakes twirl, like they're dancing high.
Sweaters are tangled, hugs filled with cheer,
As we toast to the warmth, and silly things near.

A squirrel on skis, catches our gaze,
With snow on its nose, it starts to amaze.
Then giggles erupt, with hiccuping sounds,
As we craft warm wishes, in snowy surrounds.

So let laughter bubble, like cocoa in pots,
With the chill of the night, and great giggle spots.
The fire might fade, but the joy that it brings,
Will spark a new dance, as the cool evening sings.

Silver Ferns and Gilded Ashes

In the garden, leaves shimmer, all crisp and bright,
Bouncing with laughter, in the soft moonlight.
Bunnies prance wildly, in a snowy whirl,
While kittens chase flakes, with a tangle and twirl.

Joyful whispers echo, through trees standing tall,
As giddy hearts twinkle, in laughter's great call.
A dance of the snowflakes, a twirly ballet,
As goofy creations come out to play.

Gilded ashes wink, from a fireplace frame,
With stories of snowmen, all bearing a name.
Bright lights shimmer, with a raucous delight,
Casting funny shadows, through the chilly night.

So let hearts blend, with joy in the air,
Creating warm smiles, for all those who dare.
In a world of giggles, let cherubs ignite,
With silvered fern whispers, and dreams that take flight.

Morning's Promise on a Frosted Path

Chilly toes in slippers bright,
I skated past the dog in fright.
The coffee pot's now steaming hot,
But where my keys are, I forgot.

The neighbor's cat is on a quest,
To steal my lunch—such an unfair jest!
I chase her off with quite a shout,
While snowflakes dance and swirl about.

The snowman grins with button eyes,
His carrot nose is not a prize.
He'd give a wink if he could move,
But frozen limbs don't quite improve.

As squirrels leap from tree to tree,
They plot their nutty jubilee.
In morning's glow, I can't ignore,
The frosty prank that's set in store.

Silent Whisper of Coals

In the hearth, the embers glow,
I hear them whisper secrets low.
They crackle softly, start to tease,
And take their turns at warming leaves.

The cat, convinced she's quite the queen,
Stares at the fire like it's a dream.
But when the logs let out a yelp,
She leaps and lands with quite a skelp.

The dance of flames brings silly cheer,
As marshmallows roast, we toast the year.
I dropped one in the chocolate mug,
And it left a gooey, sticky rug.

With each soft pop, I can't deny,
The warmth we share is truly spry.
Through winter's chill, we find our way,
With laughter bright, come what may.

A Soft Flicker Beneath a White Cloak

Beneath the drift, a candle glows,
It flickers gently as the wind blows.
I swore I saw a snowflake dance,
It slipped and slid, no second glance.

The garden gnome looks quite perplexed,
Dressed in snow, he's feeling vexed.
He's lost his hat, right off his head,
And now he's just a frosty spread.

The raccoon peeks out from the bush,
With winter snacks he's in a rush.
He grabs a sock, my favorite pair,
And makes off while I stop and stare.

With every soft flick in the night,
I laugh aloud at silly sights.
In every flake, a giggle hides,
As winter teases with its slides.

The Last Breath of Sunlight

As daylight fades, the sky turns peach,
The shadows stretch, they start to reach.
A squirrel performs a acrobatic leap,
While I just stumble—tripping deep.

The sun waves bye with a cheeky grin,
What happens next? Let chaos begin!
I'm bundled up, a clumsy bear,
Yet here I dance without a care.

The chimney puffs a happy plume,
While ducks parade in winter's gloom.
I throw some seed, they flap about,
As laughter fills the frosty route.

In the last light, we all unite,
Telling tales of snowy fright.
With giggles bright, the day we close,
As snowflakes fall—what fun it shows!

Shadows in the Shimmering Frost

As shadows play in chilly light,
The snowmen dance, what a funny sight!
With carrot noses stuck just right,
They wobble about, taking flight.

The puppies prance, paws in a spin,
Chasing their tails, they spin and grin.
With frosty breath, their fun begins,
At snowball fights, nobody wins!

Echoes of Heat Beneath Frozen Veils

A warm cup spills, what a mad cheer!
Hot chocolate rivers, too much to sear.
With marshmallows sailing, oh, so near,
We laugh as we paddle, nothing to fear.

The ice creams melt on the frosty ground,
Scoops of gooey joy all around.
We slip and slide, a clumsy sound,
In winter's grip, so silly we're found!

Hushed Flames Beneath a Crystal Sky

Candles flicker with a sassy glow,
They whisper secrets, just so you know.
But icy drafts make them dance and flow,
At times they tip, oh what a show!

The laughter bursts like bubbles pop,
As blankets hug, we never stop.
With jokes like snowflakes, we'll never drop,
In a cozy pile, we're all on top!

Warmth Wrapped in a Cold Embrace

In layers thick, we trudge through white,
With snowball mitts, we take our bite.
A dodge, a duck, oh what a fright,
As snowflakes twirl with pure delight!

The frosty wind gives cheeks a glow,
While laughter echoes, stealing the show.
In the chilly air, our spirits flow,
A jolly bunch, all aglow!

Silhouetted Serenity at Day's End

As shadows stretch and grow,
The cat jokes about a crow.
Winking stars begin to tease,
While squirrels dance among the trees.

A sigh escapes the chilly breeze,
A snowball fight? Just let me freeze!
The world is wrapped in cozy hues,
Hot cocoa dreams and winter snooze.

Laughter bounces off the walls,
While frost invites us for snowballs.
With funny hats and twinkling eyes,
We bid farewell to sunny skies.

Ash and Snow Entwined

A snowman made of ash and glee,
Wobbles and falls, oh silly me!
The chimney puffs, it's all a game,
As laughter dances, unashamed.

A penguin slips in frosty cheer,
Banana peels? Not welcome here!
With mittens stuck in melting blobs,
We dodge the snowballs, slyly mobs.

The flames want snowflakes for a dance,
While we just giggle at our chance.
In funny hats, we prance about,
As winter whispers, there's no doubt.

A Fragile Dance of Light and Ice

The stars play tag with frosty nights,
As fairies twirl in snowy lights.
Icicles wobble from the beams,
Making everyone burst with dreams.

An old dog wags his icy tail,
Then sneezes snowflakes, what a trail!
With jolly giggles in the air,
Hot chocolate spills everywhere.

A game of chase, we zig and zag,
As winter snorts into a rag.
We laugh so hard, our cheeks are pink,
In ice and light, we dance and wink.

The Quiet Slope of Dusk

The mountains snicker as they slide,
With snowflakes rolling down the side.
A penguin pilgrimage, what a sight,
As shadows grow and play with light.

Witty squirrels scout for fun,
While frosty fingers pinch and run.
In quiet slopes, a snowball flies,
Creating giggles and surprise.

We twirl around in frosty bliss,
Plotting schemes we can't dismiss.
As evening giggles take the stage,
Winter's antics, a silly page.

Flickers Beneath Snowy Skies

The stars are winking in a playful way,
While snowflakes twirl, and children play.
A frosty dance in jolly delight,
As sleds go flying through the night.

The moon's a cookie on a silver plate,
As snowmen giggle, it's getting late.
Hot cocoa's steaming, marshmallows in sight,
Laughter and whispers fill the night.

Penguins in hats have joined the fun,
Sliding and gliding, they're on the run.
Snowball fights turn into jolly wars,
While penguins giggle behind snowy doors.

So let's toast to fun under the moon's soft beam,
Where winter and laughter make the perfect team.
Wrapped in cozy warmth, we share a cheer,
To nights full of joy, with friends so near.

The Last Flicker of Daylight

The sun's saying bye with a quirky grin,
As shadows stretch out and the chill begins.
A squirrel in mittens, what a sight to see,
Chasing its tail like it's lost at sea.

The clouds wear pajamas, fluffy and bright,
While breezes whisper secrets of the night.
A carrot-nosed fellow strikes a silly pose,
As he pulls off his scarf, oh where does he go?

Candles are flicking in a snow-draped home,
While gingerbread men jog and start to roam.
A dance of the chairs as they twirl with glee,
Under the watch of a giddy old tree.

The day dips low but the laughter stays,
In cozy corners, where fun always plays.
Let's toast to the evening and all the cheer,
To moments of joy we create each year.

Coals Aglow in Quietude

The embers dance like little elves,
In a room where we let our laughter delve.
With snow outside forming fluffy mounds,
Inside, the joy of companionship abounds.

Roasting marshmallows, they start to sing,
As we swap stories of silly old things.
A ghost made of cocoa gives a playful fright,
While the shadows gather, ready for night.

The cat wears a scarf, oh what a sight,
Dreaming of tuna in the soft moonlight.
The coals crackle softly, a tune all its own,
While we laugh about chaos that we once sown.

In the glow of evenings, friendship ignites,
As snowflakes fall with the grace of kites.
To cozy moments that make our hearts swell,
We gather together, all's well — all's well!

The Embrace of Evening's Chill

The chill settles in with a playful tease,
As winter whispers and casts its ease.
Footprints in snow like a jigsaw puzzle,
Lead to hot cider, our warm, fizzy muzzle.

With scarves wrapped tight and cheeks aglow,
We dream of mischief beneath the snow.
A dance of the flakes in a wintery show,
While the stars pop out for a glittery glow.

A snowball fight leads to giggles and slips,
As friends tumble down, and there go the quips!
Frosty faces, with laughter in spades,
Rule the chilly night in our merry charades.

So let's cheer to the chilly air,
With friends who can cuddle and share.
With hearts so warm, and laughter so free,
We embrace the night, just you and me!

Embers in Gentle Haze

As the sky turns from blue to a gray,
A cat chases shadows and has its own play.
The mantles are warm, the cookies are near,
But Aunt Mabel's fruitcake? Oh dear, oh dear!

The flickering logs seem to dance and cheer,
While Uncle Joe snores, we try not to hear.
A marshmallow gets stuck on the dog's fur,
Now he's a treat you can't help but purr!

With giggles and snickers, we run with delight,
As sparks chase the stars in the soft, cozy night.
Who needs a fire when laughter's on high?
Let's roast these bad jokes 'til they sizzle and die!

Oh, the warmth that we make, it's more than just heat,
A melting of hearts and some sweets that we eat.
A sip of hot cocoa, a toast with our cups,
We'll giggle and wiggle and never give up!

Whispering Flakes of Dusk

The dark comes a-creeping, the snow starts to fall,
It whispers like secrets, a fuzzy white shawl.
But what's that ahead? Is it snow or a cat?
They're making snow angels, or are they just fat?

Flakes gather round, collecting on chairs,
And a snowman emerges with wobbly stares.
He's wearing a scarf that once was my sock,
Oh, he's a fine fellow who makes quite the mock!

While snowballs fly fast, and the laughter erupts,
One hit from my brother, and down I just flump!
With cheeks rosy red and a hat from the mud,
We'll stand 'til the frost bites, or till we find food!

You see, when it snows, it's a playful old game,
Our faces get wet, but we don't feel the shame.
With giggles and tumbles, our hearts are so light,
Snowflakes are fancy, but we are just right!

Glowing Ashes in Winter's Embrace

In the glow of the ember, the room's like a dream,
But my brother just farted, and now it's a meme.
While cocoa is bubbling, and cookies are bake,
Let's not talk about that, for goodness' sake!

The shadows are wiggling, the flames are a dance,
With Grandpa's old stories, we're lost in a trance.
But the dog steals a biscuit, he thinks it's a prize,
Now we're all laughing, he's got cookie eyes!

The mantle is filled with the warmth of a cheer,
And Mom's got her eye on the last slice of pear.
Yet our hearts are so full, with the joy that we share,
Watching glowing ashes squeak out a nice glare.

As the firelight flickers, we know this is bliss,
With friends all around and hot fudge to miss.
We'll skate in our socks and slip without care,
In this cozy old den, nothing else can compare!

Frosted Glimmers at Day's End

As the sun dips down, and the stars start to peek,
We dangle our feet off the porch—it's unique!
The frost has a sparkle, the world's dressed in white,
But Grandma's still hiding her snickerdoodle bite!

The chill in the air makes us giggle and run,
But ducking the snowballs is hardly real fun.
With sprigs of old laughter that tickle our toes,
We can't seem to stop as the comedy grows!

So keep those warm blankets and cocoa on high,
The snowflakes will swirl as the laughter draws nigh.
We'll weave through the shadows and dash like mad mice,
For the night is still young, and the cookies are nice!

In this frosty enchantment, with friends by the fire,
We swap all our secrets and things that inspire.
With grins all around, we forget all our woes,
In frosted glimmers where childhood joy grows!

Comfort Found in Shimmering Stillness

In the quiet hush, a sock slipped tight,
A dance with shadows, oh, what a sight.
I sip my cocoa, marshmallows afloat,
While scarves duet with a lost winter coat.

The cat's in the chair, with a snoozy grin,
Furball on duty, it's winter's best kin.
The clock ticks slowly, as laughter prevails,
While snowflakes tumble like whimsical tales.

Laughter erupts, as I trip on a shoe,
The fridge's a mountain, its snacks peek anew.
In this shimmering silence, chaos finds peace,
As I dig through the pillows, for snacks never cease.

So gather your friends, let the warmth ignite,
In this sparkling stillness, our hearts take flight.
With each clink of mugs and each giggle shared,
Let's toast to the moments, we lovingly dared!

Last Gleams of Gold and White

As day bids adieu with a wink and a grin,
The gold of the sun makes the world spin.
Chasing snowflakes as I zigzag around,
I slip on the ice, then crash to the ground.

My dog's got a plan, he's leading the chase,
With a snowball attack, he's claiming his space.
We roll in the flakes, not a worry in sight,
Laughing at shadows that dance in the light.

With hot tea in hand and a biscuit or two,
Mustaches of cream, I'm looking like you!
Yet giggles erupt as the snow starts to fall,
I'm a walking snowman, how silly, how small!

So toast to the mixed, those twinkling hues,
In the joy of the moment, there's nothing to lose.
We nest in this warmth, and the laughter won't cease,
As day turns to night, we find our sweet peace.

The Serenity of Fading Heat

As embers smolder, but laughter stays bright,
We gather 'round, warmth feels just right.
The toast of the season, a hot mug held high,
While conspiracy whispers, and squabbles go bye.

"Who stole my blanket?" echoes in glee,
As cuddly disputes make the best cup of tea.
The winter sun yawns, then waves us a cheer,
While cheeks go rosy and spirits draw near.

The frosty air tries its best to intrude,
But the giggles keep bouncing, oh, what a mood!
With socks mismatched and tales that grow bold,
We settle for snacks that "never" get old.

So here's to good fires, with friends near by sight,
In this fading heat, hearts glow with delight.
The world outside frosts, but here we stay warm,
In our cozy cocoon, a jubilant swarm!

Radiance in a Frozen World

In a glimmering state, where winter greets cheer,
Footprints like puzzles appear, oh so near.
With a snowball in hand, I'm ready to throw,
But I'm pelted by laughter, my aim's a faux pas, though!

Sleds zoom past like dreams on a spree,
While wind-whipped hats dance like sprites full of glee.
With cheeks all aglow, we venture outside,
To conquer the hills and enjoy the glide.

The neighbors declare it's crazy, this cold,
But we're busy crafting stories, both silly and bold.
With snowmen adorned in the wackiest hats,
We giggle and tease, and we fall with no spats.

So raise your mug high, let the giggles unfold,
In this frozen world, our joy we behold.
With smiles ever bright, we melt hearts today,
In the wintry embrace, we forever shall play!

Frost Flowers in the Last Glow

In evening's last dance, they prance around,
Little frosty petals, without a sound.
They giggle and twirl, on a cold, soft breeze,
Wearing ice-covered hats, as they freeze.

They tug at your socks, oh, what a sport!
Sneaky little flowers, a chilly consort.
As the orange sun slips, they chase it down,
Painting the world in their sparkly gown.

With each little step, they seem to sneak by,
Telling tall tales of the clouds in the sky.
They roll through the grass, giggling with glee,
Stealing the warmth from your cup of hot tea.

As night finally falls, they whisper and play,
Dancing in shadows where the warm sun won't stay.
Frisky and feisty, they twinkle and glow,
Frosty little jesters, putting on a show.

Vanishing Gold in the Hush of Night

Golden beams shimmer, then start to divide,
A silly old sun takes a long, silly ride.
He winks at the stars, all scattered and bright,
Then slips in his bed, whispering, "Goodnight!"

Hush falls upon earth as the day takes a snooze,
While the giggling shadows share funny old news.
A light-hearted breeze plays tricks on the pines,
While the trees shake their branches like silly designs.

Down in the garden, the gnomes have a ball,
They trip on their hats, and they stumble and sprawl.
With flickering laughter, they start a parade,
In the fading gold glimmer, their antics cascade.

So hush, little night while the world takes a rest,
Keep watch on these jests, they're simply the best.
As shadows extend and the light starts to fade,
Only the giggles of dusk shall invade.

Light's Farewell in Snow's Embrace

The last rays of sunlight, they wave with a grin,
As snowflakes come rushing, eager to begin.
With a flip and a flop, they blanket the ground,
Turning the world into laughter unbound.

Each flake tells a joke, as it twirls through the air,
Tickling your nose and the top of your hair.
With snowman creations that wobble and sway,
As they bicker and tease in a snowy ballet.

A snowball flies past, like a cheeky little brat,
And laughter erupts, oh, where's my fine hat?
As the sun bids farewell, it's a toast to the cold,
Where snowflakes remind us that laughter is gold.

So let's dance like the flurries, all jolly and bright,
Wrapped up in a quilt under twinkling stars' light.
Let the warmth fill our hearts, 'til the day comes anew,
As we cherish the giggles of this frosty debut.

Soft Shadows of the Dusk

Tiptoeing softly, the shadows appear,
With a wiggle and giggle, they bring evening cheer.
They peek from the corners, so playful, so sly,
Whispering secrets as the sun waves goodbye.

The trees wear their masks, all twisted and bent,
As shadows play hide and seek, full of intent.
They flicker like candles in a soft evening race,
Dancing in patterns, leaving no trace.

The moon starts to chuckle, all round and so bright,
Joining the clamor of the playful night.
With laughter and echoes that bounce through the air,
The shadows weave stories without a single care.

So let's join the frolic as dusk falls with grace,
Twirling through giggles in this shadowy space.
In the dance of the evening, we find our delight,
In soft, giggling shadows that steal through the night.

Echoes of Warmth in the Cold

In the chill of evening's grin,
Penguins skate, slipping thin.
A snowman sneezes, what a blast,
Sledding down, he's lost his hat.

Frosty breath makes funny shapes,
Everyone looks like a grape.
Snowball fights bring laughs galore,
Oops! I slipped, and down I bore.

Candles flicker with a dance,
Mice come out to join the prance.
Hot cocoa spills, a sugary flood,
Laughter echoes through the mud.

So gather 'round, the silly crew,
With marshmallows in the brew.
Laughter mingles with the night,
In silly warmth, we find delight.

A Celestial Fire in a Frozen Realm

Stars above begin to twinkle,
Snowflakes fall, a frozen sprinkle.
Yet here we are, a merry bunch,
Warming up with soup to munch.

A campfire made of ice and cheer,
Giggling kids come racing near.
One trips over, falls like dough,
Look at him, in the drifted snow!

Marshmallows roast with silly flair,
Every bite met with a stare.
S'mores are cracked, the chocolate's gone,
But laughter lingers, carrying on.

Beneath this frozen, starlit dome,
We find joy in every home.
Though the cold tries to stake its claim,
Our funny hearts always stay the same.

The Mellow Glow of Winter's Hearth

By the fire, the shadows play,
A cat who thinks he knows the way.
Chasing tails of friendly light,
Bouncing here, then out of sight.

Grandma's knitting, dropping stitches,
Grandpa's telling ghostly witches.
But all the tales are full of jest,
Warming hearts, we know it best.

The hot tub bubbles with a cheer,
Snowmen watch with frosty sneer.
A bird who stole a cookie crumb,
Flies off quick, oh what a bum!

In this mellow, cozy space,
Laughter sprinkles like a lace.
As shadows dance 'round the bright light,
We chuckle softly at the night.

Fading Flame and Frost's Caress

Flames flicker low, a final glow,
Time for bed, but not just so!
Cupcakes stacked with icing tall,
Who knew snow could melt them all?

With puffy coats and silly hats,
We race outside like crazy rats.
Slipping, sliding, here and there,
Oops! I fell, I'm in despair!

But laughter rolls upon the ground,
As I catch snowflakes all around.
Frosty friends throw tricks and jibes,
Even the moose are full of scribes!

Beneath the stars, the cold can't bite,
With giggles shared, all feels just right.
A fading flame, but hearts are warm,
In this frosted, funny charm.

A Tapestry of Warmth and Frost

In mittens I trudge, my feet oh so cold,
The snowflakes dance wildly, as I laugh and scold.
Hot cocoa's my armor, a sip, then a spill,
Dodging snowballs fired with expert skill.

The sledding hill calls, oh the giggles arise,
I land in a bush, what a comical surprise!
With frosty red cheeks and a grin ear to ear,
I declare winter's magic, my laughter sincere.

Snowmen are built with a scarf and a grin,
But one with a carrot? That's what I call sin!
Yet we share laughs, as he leans with a flair,
A snowman in pajamas? What a ridiculous pair!

So let the snow fall, let the candied dreams flow,
I'll dance in the flakes, in my funny snowshow.
Each chilly mishap a gem to unfold,
In this frosty adventure, the warmth never grows old.

Whispers of Fire in a Wintry Realm.

The crackling logs hum a humorous tune,
As I roast marshmallows, the dog makes a swoon.
With chocolatey fingers, I munch on my snack,
But who knew that marshmallow gets stuck on my back?

A blanket of snow, all fluffy and bright,
I slip and I slide in the shimmering light.
My friends all around, with snowballs in tow,
We strategize plans for a flurry of show.

We launch through the air, our giggles a ring,
A snowball finds me, oh what joy it can bring!
But the laughter can echo, in the fiercest of chills,
As we tumble in heaps, our whimsy fulfills.

In the glow of the hearth, I can't help but dream,
Of party hats made from soft winter cream.
We dress up the night with some glitzy decor,
And dance to the flames, as we whistle and roar.

Embers in the Dusk

As the sunset blushes, a mission begins,
To gather the wood with laughter and grins.
But my friends drop the logs, they stumble and fall,
And I roar with giggles, I'm having a ball!

Around the warm fire, we weave silly tales,
Of snowmen with dreams and ambitious penguin trails.
The embers are bright, a confetti of light,
We toast to the mayhem, as the stars shine bright.

Marshmallow mishaps, they roast to a crunch,
In a food fight frenzy, we see who can punch.
With gooey delights that stick to the face,
Who knew snowy nights could lead to such grace?

So let the warmth linger, as the night takes its flight,
We're a band of misfits, oh what a sight!
With laughter and cheer, through the cool evening air,
In the glow of the fire, our humor laid bare.

Whispering Husk

Beneath a blanket of soft, snowy fluffs,
We huddle together, oh where's all the stuff?
A party of friends, with laughs in our boots,
But missing the snacks? Oh gosh, what a hoot!

With whispers of warmth that flicker and play,
The fireplace crackles, and we dance in our sway.
Our feet take us spinning, in giggles we nest,
Creating a whirlwind of joy—just the best!

The hot springs are calling, but first we must dare,
To leap in the snow while forgetting our care.
Oh plop! In a puddle of sloshy delight,
We'll burrow in laughter till the morning light.

So here's to the evenings of warmth and of cheer,
With frost on our noses and snacks drawing near.
We'll gather the tales of our hilarious plight,
Whispering soft jokes as we hold the night tight.